Rai

MW01615558

by Charlotte Shell

 HOUGHTON MIFFLIN   BOSTON

PHOTOGRAPHY CREDITS: Cover © Workbook Stock/Jupiter Images; Toc © Workbook Stock/Jupiter Images;
2 © Masterfile Royalty Free; 3 © Photographers Choice Photography/Veer; 4-5 © Workbook Stock/Jupiter Images;
6 © Alloy Photography/Veer

Printed in China

ISBN-13: 978-0-547-01845-4
ISBN-10: 0-547-01845-2

6 7 8 9 0940 15 14 13 12
4500358728

Here is the sun.

Here is the cloud.

Here is the rain.

Here is the lightning.

Here is the rainbow!

Responding

✔ TARGET SKILL **Sequence of Events** This book is about a rainy day. What happens in the sky first? What happens next? What happens last?

Talk About It

Text to Self Draw a picture that shows something you did on a rainy day. Tell a story about it. Remember to tell what happened in the beginning, middle, and end.

7

✔ **TARGET SKILL** **Sequence of Events** Tell the order in which things happen.

✔ **TARGET STRATEGY** **Analyze/Evaluate** Tell how you feel about the text, and why.

GENRE **Informational text** gives facts about a topic.